The Sink House

JULIA WILLIAMS

Amanda + Glenn + Kaelan + Maddy + Mr B.
I am very special and important

Auntie Julia

Love,

Julia

COACH HOUSE BOOKS

Published with the assistance of the Canada Council for the Arts and the Ontario Arts Council. We also acknowledge the financial support of the Government of Ontario through the Ontario Book Publishing Tax Credit Program and the Government of Canada through the Book Publishing Industry Development Program (BPDIP).

Canada Council for the Arts   Conseil des Arts du Canada   ONTARIO ARTS COUNCIL CONSEIL DES ARTS DE L'ONTARIO   Canadä

LIBRARY AND ARCHIVES CANADA CATALOGUING IN PUBLICATION

Williams, Julia, 1976 –
    The sink house / Julia Williams. – 1st ed.
Poems.
ISBN 1-55245-146-1
    I. Title.
PS8645.I45S55 2004   C811'.6   C2004-903774-9

for Dan

wave:

save nothing but you
what stays is staid
this is our motto

photo captions: a flood starts somewhere

1   *here comes water*
2   *flesh*
3   *tourists love riverbanks*
4   *gradual adjustment in clothing and attitude*
5   *creeping doubt. was that the flood?*
6   *dam*
7   *domestic tragedy*

statement of parts

all that belonged to we discarded
all that belonged to we split down
the middle parted like hair the red sea our ways

we lifejacked
I can't guarantee

all that belonged to we paid for
fist over hand to mouth to foot
all that belonged to we broke

we categorically deny
have no room
have no rooms

all that belonged to we exploded
under the flood inside out, out

we sink
so swim

this reminds me of a story about
vegetables around the time my
mother stopped wearing bathing suits
around the time we ate fresh peas and
carrots straight from the garden
which exploded in the water

all that belonged to we froze
lightbulb filament popped and sparked

did I even see this with my eyes

we submit

all that belonged to we soaked and fell in perfect pieces

gasp

the street inches closer

swoosh, settle
cars pass
rubber boots, swans
a gasping street

snatch photos
firemen and sandbags
waves at the welcome mat
brown tiles, blue sitting room
all those books

hands wringing wet

upstairs chairs, throws
dried flowers
bedroom an ark

a stripped room
we park on high stools
because of the inches
because of the doorjamb
because careful

our

your fingers, newsprint
clean white corners
double joints, long thighs

an eye for balance

dry skin at my cheeks and ankles
how you rushed matters
my cheek lost your shoulder
I caught your tear on my tongue

the sink

what a trick
you walled in
the ceiling sags, sandbagged
front door a cave

and all windows, shards

binliner to floodline the front path
sharks in the kitchen sink

I wish I had
we wish it hadn't
this is my doing

stinking river. we expected

those rugs of yours, tugboats
this tidal barrier
sandbag, a feeder
osmotic tension, balance
a voice on the floodline: worry

14

call this space diffused
no peeking
my trick walled you in

I came here to wallow in starfish

exclusion

guard welcome mats, hoard sandbags

when the bank bursts tonight every space will be relevant
gather paper, chairs, rugs: become hermetic

a draught excluder excludes nothing moist
curtains leak sunlight
roll down the windows to equalize sunlight, to get out

why complain when the season turns on us?

navigation

Home from work, straight as the crow flies, I begin to think direction from above. Made Oxford a bus route, a map, long before north and south ease apart. Tourists ask directions. I'm weathered, I'm resident.

Town centre in a fingerpoint, an arrow, we stamp times on restaurants and sharp corners. Two layers: the edgy geography like last Christmas, all underwater.

what colour does grass grow in England?

Roads converge like knuckle skin or kite lines, like hedges or pinwheels branching from High Street like your little town. We never left the garden, flowered and bowered, a knot in a string of street.

Calgary's suburbs designed this way, corkscrews and carriage wheels, culs-de-sac, the houses older than all the trees.

measure us

measure that first winter
a ruler, eked points
soap grain on fabric

a concrete bridge, thick rails
space to spy on city centre

Oxford, Calgary settled by rail
ox trains, wet buffalo hooves
freshwater stained by swans and geese

measure us

that first winter: brown, blue
cold loomed, a gargoyle

envy us both for our sheer dumb luck

does this sound hollow to you?

18

the first regret

I liked this bridge
lonely for mountain stone, stone

refracts bees and midges
eats sunlight and looms over the river
shakes with occasion

I liked this moss
creeping between stones like mortar

I never once saw the bridge from its side
or paused, crossed the humped spine
on wet, steady feet

sharp

Even a flood gets boring week after week. Water dulls
every edge and all the knives have crumbled. In the
garden fish pick their teeth, even crabs. I've lost interest
in lampreys and barnacles. Gravity works sideways
underwater, nothing weighs anything anymore. Whirl
my arms, swirl the migrating salmon, trout, minnows,
fissures. These knifeblades grow lacy, floral, nothing for
it but a swim, a snooze, a lap. All punches pulled down
here, velocity won't work and nothing crashes, nothing
bangs or jars, blood can't flow but clouds. I'm sick of
vibration. A flood evens week after week, smoothes
out, grows over, narrow, gentle, boring.

This is a hole, every eye rolled back in every head.
Blades aren't steel underwater, they're silt.

the street

Our small corner soaked, floating. Outdoors, edges are fur, streetlights spark and flicker. This street trails a creek, creeps around corners and melts sandbags. In this box beams expose. This street creaks like an ancient river, wooden boards raft feet. Who needs a ferry when oars just sink. Every bicycle becomes a slice, chain links a weed net. Marigolds become fish. Every car wakes me.

Corners sharpen inside and a fist won't fit, can't contract. This street becomes a bed and creeps to the door, ruffles sandbags, becomes a sound. Beams expand, snug, fingers box. A river gains angles, a mattress, a rush.

old habits

we used to say we owned too many candles.
mud bakes in a ginger sun
reflected. one finger in this small hole
means no dice, dammit. damn it
we'll eat sandbags for dinner if
we must. grass used to grow
on the roof, long before water dissolved
these walls and stranded us without
dishes to wash or wallpaper.
mud fakes a pressure under sun
refracted, bent. around these forks
spoons a silver service all tarnished
crystal gone to rust. these trees grew
puckered when the water backfired.

blazon

You made the bed, petalled the pillows. Each light bulb hums, dim and seasonless. I hadn't expected a floral arrangement, just stripes or squares, paisley or polygons. Dry carpet grain, vacuum tracks, taut tucks at each corner. Curls of wallpaper, terry slippers. I am silled. This view is prejudiced, adjusted. Light threads my arms and slices my hair:

The sill flatters me, frames me, each toe splayed against whitewash. No glass in these eyes. You locked door and wardrobe, drawer and chest. You have made the bed, nails half-hammered to catch cheeks and elbows, sawdust sucked by a termite, a hoover. I didn't expect flowers but silk substitutes, stalks grass-like, lacy. A suitable sill, a tangle of two-by-four.

I understand dust now. From all of these angles.

salvage

what to salvage when the whole road sinks:

sigh. are we bored
or waiting
measure our feet and fingers

upstream, firemen fish for a house
to salvage

tepid air, a relief
raindrops cease so I can walk
without feeling under siege
underwater

a molten house
I ask you
we steel ourselves
(I imagine books, not wires)

the kitchen peels back to reveal
entire centuries
a dining service too wide
for this street

too heavy to salvage
too hideous to throw back

a rescue so very, very severe

the flood was so funny

when your house sank I salvaged a soap boat. you were
on the news in your yellow dingy I heard but the TV
was wet.

buckets sank first. you thought this ironic in your
skipper hat and sloshing galoshes.

neighbours scrapped for sandbags, firemen wound
around lightpoles, chased by frothing bathbombs.

we still expected snow. this is the litmus test, you said
and wedged paper around the door.

a river shapes itself. *but this is me speaking*

you took a nautical line and anchored aweigh. for
amusement we flushed all the toilets but nothing
could buoy us.

no joke: all my notes dissolved. all our skeins keeled.

house:

tap tap
attar of roses
shakes awake
tin shingles
tip

photo captions: inestimable property damage

1 *prise apart*
2 *fork, hammer, tablecloth*
3 *makeshift comforts, specific accidents*
4 *salt*
5 *failed adhesives (true disaster)*
6 *grim lips*
7 *string*

fanciful

I left out:
snowbank, alarmclock, birthmark
a perfect stack of books

you don't look right
we're too close, pressed in this bed
I can't stand us
come back inside
you'll fall in the river and drown

take this photo
there's a poem in here
if we stretch our lips far enough

look at me making fancy
a cold streak
art is like that; love is like

oh, who will believe us
sugared over
this page is salt flavoured
(but you live at the back of my tongue)

take this photo
scrape off the paint
a string along
an ice point: *I describe you*

distance

rings wake me but the line
crackles, can you hear?
beside ourselves

this is your letter folded
bent a line at a time

non-linear, winged speed
can't we wake together

I thought space favoured us
you're breaking up

remember we saw ourselves in the river
speed compensates, but slowly

the furniture

sandbags leach the doorstep
we phone for supper
so the bell pops from its socket
no time to think river but from the second floor
bedroom puzzled with tables
we run up- and downstairs like water

all night the window cracks
fissures like handles
we phone the floodline
frost in the toilet is warning enough
wallpaper strips from the ceiling
this is called dry rot

we spot orange at the baseboard
call it rust
upstairs chess a bed with CDs
stripes can be simple
if wallpaper over the window
muffles the rush

history

Oxford all puddled
a mapless accident
your stained terrace
we balanced on ice skin
outside your green door
your pipes, your drapes
mark your coming and going
your mind making

Calgary snow flattened
a fingering sun
one stained pane
it's simple here, more solid
glassed in
I love you, I said: but sound changes
in thin air
Calgary arid, glacial dust
between walls

we trace our steps
sheeted by rain, mud
swans and geese
my dried daffodils

mostly my patch of earth
a trace of you in a corner
only a shade in the wood

the cupboard

no bubbles under those eyes
a wink speaks volumes more
than a tear, at least a bubble
shows breath

shut the door

cyclic strains of oopsy daisy
through this murky cupboard
shut the door, the eyes
hide the blister pack

maintenance

frames were never wood enough
an architect assigned to
change these screens
clogged with dust and dry bees
a backyard beige
a squirt of soap is all it takes
sometimes a bucket weighs on us

a carpenter to veil the porch
with wire nests and gingham
pocked and squared away
to quit the buzzing underneath
a brisk whisk is all it takes
sometimes a handle splinters
a task weighs on us

pipes won't be plugged nor stung
a plumber was invited
to open tubes and squares
bees are unsussable and lately
we suspect soft noises
a clasped fist is all it takes
to bear us up

leak

all my life I thought keys were keys

I thought critically

what can I say of seven years in a cell

a slat underwater, a niagara box

these gaps implicate me

what is seven years but a stunt

all my life I called a trick a trick

a thin trickle says sealant is porous

walls bend and angle my posters

but this is not criticism

I could be less happy, less homey

I could draw on my legs and carve scales in my forearms

all my life the window bubbled

the sealant poured

forgetting the flood

face us: I came all this way for

colour. a city that spreads.

road dust spins in Calgary

and chokes out crow's feet.

well, this is how you find

lost keys. *this is how*

you disappear.

dry:

scrape dust
to remember fruit
to drown head first

photo captions: a series of small breaks

the post-mortem

such a crisp poem

she is convinced she can haul up this ricked
scarred sink house

we had to do this: drape our capes around
larger pictures, meatier questions
(cull is not the same as kill)

so sweet in bed with you, such flattery
such selective fiction

the getaway

croissants when I craved fresh pear
we photographed food
snapped up wallpaper
dived through balcony doors

my arches blistered

croque monsieur, cuppa
we crowed, such distance
abnormal vowels
and frogs, ha ha
you put your face on my belly

my cold woke us
photographed through tines
forehead to glass
to hear a canal slide

pompidou, sacre coeur, good idea!
love cobbles, stones
bridges and escalators
we did everything right
skipped the right views
and detours

five drownings

She makes up colours because she remembers in greyscale. Consults him for details, textures, can't match his eye for materials. The first time she touched him her fingers changed. *What did you think of my face back then?* She makes organs out of cells, stretches his patience. He dyes her bed blue and when she crawls in on cold nights she thinks she's underwater.

Keeps her clothes on. Doesn't start when rusty water
bashes through old taps and stains her shoes. Shoes fit
like skin. Shoes fall in the sea, cross the island, dry
strung from basement rafters. Perhaps the house rattles
her. She sweeps dead flies off chairs, drops flies over the
porch rail. Each morning she forgets which country
she's in. Strokes her belly flat again.

She tells him she researched this creek and he says where did you get those blisters? *Cheer up, it's still possible everyone will drown.* She admits she made the flood sound deeper than it was. He wonders where she lost her shoes, how she gathered leech rings around her ankles.

Sure a person can drown in half an inch of water, but an ocean makes it easy.

She excuses the pouches around her eyes as dampness. If pressed, she'll convince him she slept well that first week, seaweed bunched around her feet and woven through her toes. *No, the rain did not dismay me.* Rain compliments grey buildings and roads. Still, she cries her way through the dye on her pillowcase and stains her cheeks blue.

harvest

leaf and tunnel tide-rounded
suddenly

uprooted, a premature season
peapods burst, carrots
thyme, cauliflower melts
like lard, like ice
cream, like dust

the next day

measure us here like
that first summer
air baked dry
barren shadows through October

until our mouths cracked
sky looms, leans
presses our ribcages

good morning
yellow flowers
are raining from our hedges

the flood

these examples hold no water
but a life is worth documenting
piece by piece

for example: *I'm not worried*

water slides up the street
snaps out window panes

this house is material
grit, watermarks, bedspreads
daffodils and porch rails
clean this story

for example: holes can be mended

retain memory, water
produce this document

the house ends, this yard beds a river

it rains and my eyes sting
it rains all over this house
and this house is over

wet:

wave at banks
wake underwater
here fish are woven with leaves

photo captions: attack from all angles

flood topography

1. This creek's made its bed. Feathers, scales, fins. Deep down it feels like cooled rice. Sharp. Sharper.

2. Pebbles were always boulders. Were always mountains. This creek pares down, squares up, bends around.

3. A wide puddle or a river a string a twig a hair.

4. Walkable creek, too cold but heating, too leached but clearing. Mostly unfished.

5. Call the creek motley or wizened. Turns to much too chilly an undertow too gentle for a swan. Even a goose would seek a river.

6   How about a lake bed. A feeder, parent, tribu-
    tary. How about an ode or elegy, an epigraph
    for this creek.

7   Creek sand never leaves a boot toe. Never less
    than grey red stones. Sun bent through water
    on a clear day.

8   Three islands carved humps or hummocks.
    Treeless, weedless, sandbarred, too rocky for
    bare feet. Too creeky for bear feet.

9   *More a leak than a body.*

drought

false bridge for a dry creekbed
all undergrowth in an overgrown country

when the river burst last christmas
the island drowned

sweet and damp beneath
the train bridge

water carved by engines
a single orange light in dead dark

daffodils kitty-corner
a crocus purple graveyard

ground steps, dank sewage
a new book smell

remember, I was middle class
I wanted these: books, bicycles
all this wood and glass
stitched to small families in my palms

now when I smell wet brass

so eager
so minor

flight

stow your grief, separate the tarmac. semaphore
reminds me of flying. can you pass a metal detector
without a twang?

flood animals

1   This creek makes a string makes up the distance
    turns on me every time dial tones.

2   Water cords us together binds us hand and foot
    the tenor of our voices, follicles, fingerprints,
    hair wringing with rain.

3   Deepens past the suspension bridge so murky
    last spring that leech on your ankle a turned
    vein.

sealegged

a lost continent stays lost
define aquatic: airless
every ship rots
all artifacts are dangerous
define pirate: eyepatch
cannons moss at the mouths
what angle the sail
what ballast, what rig
nobody fits in a crow's nest
or fixes a breaker

flood recipes

1 This creek is a door hinge on your accent your vowels and dropped consonants.

2 Ahh, haitch, strung up like caught fish.

3 Where the creek widens sound amplifies.

4 Two of us hunker down clapped together under thunder.

5 We eat sandwiches pick saskatoon berries for pies and I'm soaked through skin and bone.

6 What lives in a creek is what seals surface tension.

7 These little leeches like raisins fragmented and hunted by fish.

current

I thought I knew what a river did
I misunderstood
missed the flood
the taste of water

(whatever a break is)

duck under when the wave heaves
to break surface from below
to make a waterhole

I don't believe you just fell through
not with that saw in your hand

upset this water table
you told me rivers healed themselves
explain this tinny taste

(whatever a dam does)

irrigation pipe
means every vein and trough is edible
means all water is damned

If you think ice is liquid
hand me a glass
this is what we do with water around here

swing that hammer from the shoulder
this is what we do with dams around here

don't let these arms fool you
there is no procedure
for waving and drowning

the false floods

don't follow me unless you mean to wade this creek
deep as a mouth wide as the sea the chance of you
catching me so, so small

tell me the one about uprooted daffodils and hail like
fists belting the roof until sunrise

I had a dream our hedges were flattened

tell me about the clammy swimming pool out back
that froze you swim faster stuck in place

the flood got so boring

pests drift from the creek
puffballs, mildew

blame the flood, of course
the mixed-up landscape
(I could say 'washed away' but mean rinsed, eroded)

a flood dug these fissures
sucked up the grass
(floated you away, I'd say
but your face shows in the water)

sun blisters the painted sill
it's raining in England
confused by heat, reassured by telephone

I expect you

ho-hum, afternoon
minnow, ripple, raft

fish

fragments, what colourful trees, the high sky crackles:
skeins to hold water, shapes to fit given shapes, frag-
ments gonged by waves, belly up

two feet low beat, two wooden flippers, call for drinks
and bring them to bear on this mad creek, so shallow

broken water snapped for surface tension, we wriggle
under mounds of silver scales

what weighs the loss inflicted by a dam: *oh, you heft all
buckets, you resist all tides*

wreck:

anchor, remind my body
refract through water
this unshipped rudder
soft bark. water oil salt
ebb

photo captions: hideous natural hazards

1. *toothy beasts, unbroken water*
2. *submersion, suffocation, containing edible air*
3. *killer animals*
4. *tooth gnashing*
5. *the flood!*
6. *a little death*

strategy

fish only fly to escape certain death

we lack speed, use surprise
waves are simple and soft
sinking is strategy
not suffocation

at sea sextant holds off disaster

cold compass for each hand
birds won't eat from my palm
they're worried by damp
and murderous fish

invasions

freshwater bound
we bruise like fruit

bright fishes flank
us, plastic shards

bankside gravel
bars, jellyfish

caught under glass
or crackling shrimp

salty hair, dried
grains on our thighs

red welts blacken
underwater

camouflage

lobe coral
hides

crackling shrimp

night hides
octopus, caves
hide seaturtle

lobe coral
yields

antler coral

fish slide
sea cucumbers
sand fissures

invisible hunters, thumbnail squid
underwater speaking is just
vibration, underwater we clap
our hands to explain simple
dangers

lobe coral
hides

eels, depths shelter
giants

risk

what is frightening about water

1   water is a dank and fusty old woman who serves
     stale biscuits and real human flesh, tells
     tedious stories of ghosts and sea monsters
2   water responds to no whim but its own,
     squeezing itself into glasses and eyedroppers,
     bending straight lines into beams

what is frightening about fish

1   fish are compelled by primitive instincts,
     swaying seahair and holding fins in provocative
     poses
2   fish cook completely in less than two minutes,
     a tang undisguised by lemon, garlic and ladles
     of turmeric

memorize this for the sake of clarity
measure it for definition
these are your own dangers, after all
nerves soothed by the slap of wet fins on water

record

The best explanation of flood is a series of snapshots.
This is an exchange of vows.
This is a dance. The best way to control death.
Is a series of snapshots. Narrow sheets.
In small boxes. Faces pared for film.

Hot mud marks the edge of the world.
Where waves rise like buildings. Boats.
Stop dead. A bridge here wouldn't span.
Such distance. Would buckle when the water.
Surged.

carving

The only cure for sea monster is dismemberment.
Carry a cleaver and an oar. Let the monster's.
Fibre guide you, and cut against the grain.
This makes it tender. Consume the heart.
All warriors do.

inexplicable flood

windows are heated sand

if you dig deep enough
windows are heated sand
in certain beaches
your feet boil

had she been wrecked

no earthly explanation
had she been wrecked or burned
there would be bodies
would be debris

a skeletal hump of feathery paper
useless objects faded grey
dark green streaks on the horizon
a catastrophe measured in knots

explanation

caskets washed through
mangrove knots oblong
waterlogged barnacled
rough dissolved men

stone-faced medusa
a perishing raft
survivors were ghosts
they ate human remains

wine water flour
perished wood
torn bodies
cooked with fish

a giant squid
rabies pirates

this is a list of probable causes
a theory of absence
a cure for frustration

an earthly explanation

lung

scarabs and oil men
blink at the sky
which is always blue

city grows here despite
scale and weed

we live on shifting grass
caught in ropes of sea kelp
squeezed breathless

our eyes don't line up
cities are based on triangles
cities are built like hedrons

we should be sailors
no taste for knots

if our eyes were parallel
you'd remember breathing
food is so salty here

tastes like the edge of the world

the deeper deep

a nasty accident
so unromantic, a hollow hull

not a wreck but a reef
painted with nudibranches
murky gaps stuffed with polyps
and phosphorescent coral digits

clear water bends distance
shark skin is made of teeth

a creature made of teeth
sheds teeth

shedding teeth

rock, whale, gale, sea monster
ice, albatross, broken teeth

dog-faced scourge of the deep
eyes roll inward, tortured by fishermen

little lemon shark, shedding teeth
hunts castaways through steel and ice

seal-faced shark, in our belly
recovered potatoes, plastic, soup tins

an undigested dolphin, coils of rope
gnawed into nests

denticles

we thought these teeth were dragons' tongues
petrified thunderbolts

a murdered shark
vomits its stomach inside out
manifests trauma
indefensible, sharp habitat

false reef sealed
to a vertical deck

86

sea monster

placoid scales, denticles
angle along the velvet dogfish
the angular roughfish
forms a prickly shark
ripped into galuchat
upholstery, a strong fabric
used to abrade shipwood
wrapped around living room chairs

cataclysmic, dead sea scales
a collapsed riverbank littered
with broken fish

does any of this remind you of
a waterglass or a sealed lock?

cyanide fisherman

for every tide a barrier
frozen fish, bathtub sized

spouts of fresh poison
make grey ghosts of fan coral

a paralyzed octopus clenched
to a wreck

the swift ugly deaths
of all legless things

abroad

Absent across how many miles of sea monsters? Steady whitecaps, wisps on decks, mad sailors, deadheads, denticles. Bloated, dismembered, sun-baked. A magnified confinement, expanded to span a whole sea.

abroad 2

The flood rehydrates dried monsters, brightens their wet eyes and slippery fins. There are drawings of old monsters, dog-headed with teeth for skin. Monsters splash up the stairs, slap untidy tails on dissolving walls. We resist monsters, ignore sea smell. Tangled in kelp forest, we free ourselves with deadly blades and brilliant stratagems:

a möbius we
tightroping the sea

remarkable

measure us through water
refracted into angles
measure into containers
marked by stone, snow, daffodil

measure our use
each other, our narrative logic
our inherent value

measure us through rain sheets
 a backroom of
buffed turtle shells, stuffed fish

stone, wood, glass brass
a fingertip affair
we sheltered under every
sort of tree

this is a story of shape-shifting
of vessel versus content
of unseasonal, unbearable wreckage

hazard

landlocked people
make poor guides

block your ears with water
this will help you to see

if you know enough
you can navigate in rain
if you know what to do

you can predict floods
by watching salt dry
on the palms of your hands

bird flight, fish scales, tides

landlocked people just follow leaders
they do not understand these hazards
they are ungenerous, complacent

easily destroyed by a flood

float:

two river inches
net and bob
buckle yourself
the heart collapses when it stops

photo captions: summations, lost puzzle pieces

aftermath

rain stings my eyes
a city acidic and soggy
my raincoat dissolved

firemen refit window panes
seams in broken glass
brown, curling walls
wood rot, shingles, nails

this reminds me of flinging dead flies
off a balcony rail:

a beach scarred with bleached trees
green crabs beneath each stone
salt-coated teeth

I was angered by the drainspout
the reminder, the rust

surfacing

the wake lulls out candles
keep low
watch for corpses under the keel
nobody expected water

watch for deadheads, eddies
weathervanes to punch holes
in a hull
this shell is unsinkable
curl up

nobody expected weather
watch for icefloes, igloos

this damp pretends expansion
but every hull rattles
each wave shows its weave

invisibility

a fog-padded street
we should disappear
press snow to our teeth
sort our books

your photos of my ring fingers
arrows at the tips
dodging puddles and sinkholes
you insisted we shut that gap
the bridge arch swallowed

we paired off, bridged
streets formed lines between us
countries before we met

rain is stupid here
it suffocates fires
hisses down the street
a garden of clouds
our bodies watertight
to sink us

the wreck

I hate this doldrum
dead in the water
sunk by a foot, two feet
planted in water means stand or drown

the trappings of rescue
we launched unfettered
by oarlocks unburdened
by meals or treats
salted to the calves, I hate

these weeds bent over the edges
bow from starboard
sea and sky
when night rolls in I lose my hands
we lose my hands, we're lost

this depth at our own hands
by our own admission

this rescue trap
bent over the edge, sick

I hate the stretch of afternoon, midnight
food and drink, water and up

danger

What we think is the smell of chlorine is really.
The smell of ammonia on human skin.

I seem to be troubled by narrative strain.
Consecutive images push to form patterns.
Straight lines emerge despite my best efforts.
To tangle.

The best shapes are slippery.

These lines are too concerned with suffocation.
Small injuries. Perhaps we are worried.
About small animals, shark teeth, serrated.
Glass. Obviously we think we can materialize.
Heat, we can translate the occult into.
Pretty speech.

landscaping

moisture, pasture, sheep and cow

coal-stained towers daffodil frilled

nasal burn, tar and oil

the street that raised you

dusk, hummock, ground squirrel

the auto grind, lawnmower, sprinkler

the smell of damp earth

still water

visits

airport bricks are harsh, brisk
sick from salt and thin air
leather and hand lotion
flap your arms
greet me through sliding doors
you appear like a fish behind glass
and I track your wake

this sheet on my face
to spite you
to ward off flies

walked here in tight shoes
here to peek under my clothing
I've turned against you

against flies
your eyes, your eyes
wires
minnows

flood archeology

in ten thousand years a shoe
will emerge from bog mud
cracked, seamy leather
unlaced and tiny

this used to be bogland
far as the eye goes

what passes for history passes
tense never changes
a shoe still means teapot
pan, whisk
hat means belts and soupbowls

what grew here, what grows
never could mould a shoe
never could dig it

this was bogland
a house, a garden

why this shoe is tiny, only
this shoe caught off guard
ten thousand years in the drying

record

a roll of you overexposed
bleached by light

lately the living room
smells of old salt
mugs stick to shelves

we develop cheap photos
replace beech with pine
ceramic for plastic

your head spins in that photo

I've traced this map by hand
finger by finger, refolded
I've strained to remember flavours
the smell of these photos

I wish I lived near a river
I'd listen for fish
shades of green, I'd tell you
grey in the shallows

so I'd have a tracer
a dotted line to straighten me
an arrow to follow my boat

to keep my coordinates
your crosshairs

bone structures

vaulted roof
garish bone

stairs are falls
a cup to drain
a river
a teaspoon

I've become a splash

bone frames
squeaky stairs
dry is a statement
so let's drink

dark and corners
a parchment teabag
air in my bones swells
a pocketed marrow
an aerated tube

the wake in the attic wakes us
we thought I'd adjust

over

colder than Calgary
I slipped on crisp grass

if we learned one thing from the flood

I wouldn't speak to you
for walking too fast
grass grown over our feet
we tracked a canal

bristle, scrub trees, sundown

we smoothed it over
stiff water, over

about the author

Julia Williams writes poetry and fiction. She has lived in England and New Zealand, and recently returned to Calgary with her husband, Dan Mitchell. She's a former editor of *filling Station Magazine*, and the current president of the *dANDelion Magazine* board. This is her first book.

acknowledgements

I wouldn't have written *The Sink House* if Aritha van Herk hadn't encouraged me to pursue writing, and I wouldn't have wanted to be a writer if Calgary's writing community weren't so interesting and supportive. I wouldn't have come up with the idea for *The Sink House* if my friend Kathryn Leak's main floor hadn't been flooded by the Thames one Christmas. My book wouldn't have been any good without initial feedback from Fred Wah and the students of his 494 workshop, as well as the considerable influence and editing of Jill Hartman. It wouldn't have been published if Nicole Markotić hadn't bullied me into mailing to Coach House Books, and it wouldn't have become a book if Coach House hadn't done me the honour of accepting, designing and printing it. It wouldn't be coherent if not for the attentive editing of Jay MillAr and Alana Wilcox, and it wouldn't look so sharp if Darren Wershler-Henry hadn't put such effort into designing it, or if Jenny Conway-Fisher were not so visually talented. I've been very grateful for the support of my friends and family. *The Sink House* wouldn't be a love poem if I didn't know Dan Mitchell.

Typeset in Documenta
Printed and bound at the Coach House
on bpNichol Lane, 2004

Cover image by Jenny Conway-Fisher
Designed by Darren Wershler-Henry

Coach House Books
401 Huron Street rear on bpNichol Lane
Toronto, Ontario
M5S 2G5
416 979 2217 • 1 800 367 6360
mail@chbooks.com
www.chbooks.com